inspirations

DECOUPAGE

Over 20 decorative projects for the home

inspirations

DECOUPAGE

Over 20 decorative projects for the home

JOSEPHINE WHITFIELD

PHOTOGRAPHY BY ADRIAN TAYLOR

LORENZ BOOKS
NEW YORK · LONDON · SYDNEY · BATH

This edition is published in 1997 by Lorenz Books

Lorenz Books is an imprint of
Anness Publishing Inc.
27 West 20th Street
New York, NY 10011

ISBN 1 85967 431 3

Publisher: Joanna Lorenz
Editor: Clare Nicholson
Photographer: Adrian Taylor
Designer: Caroline Reeves
Illustrator: Madeleine David

Printed and bound in Hong Kong

1 3 5 7 9 10 8 6 4 2

CONTENTS

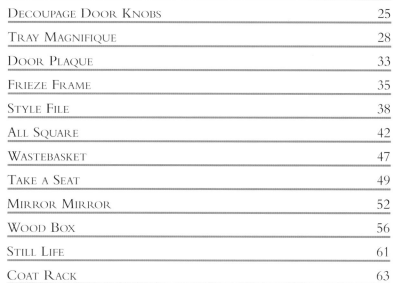

INTRODUCTION

The dictionary definition of decoupage is the cutting out and application of paper cutouts to surfaces. The process is very simple and intensely relaxing. I can easily see why decoupage became a pastime for genteel young ladies, as it is similar in its intricacy to delicate embroidery. I recently attended a course on decoupage and it was so enjoyable working in a group where moments of talk, when we all showed each other our work in progress, were interspersed with long periods of calm, as we quietly snipped and stuck down our decoupage images. The wonderful part about decoupage is that you can pick it up and put it down easily, and that even if you and a friend start with the same designs you will both end up creating something with a different feel.

A lot of the designs for decoupage are based on heavy floral designs of the Victorian era. These have their place but you should not feel constrained by them because you can use any type of paper and a whole range of images. In this book we have brought decoupage up-to-date and have taken it in a more modern, broader view. With over 20 projects for every area of your home, we have used different materials, from black-and-white prints and reproductions of famous paintings to color photocopies of flowers and interesting shapes cut out of colored paper. There are also many interesting paint techniques involved in the projects. There are clear step-by-step instructions showing how to decorate your walls, furniture and accessories. Start by simply creating a door plaque with motifs from wrapping paper. You will then be ready to tackle the larger projects, such as the stool that is transformed with multicolored squares of handmade paper. There are informative, complete materials and techniques sections.

I hope this book inspires you to take up your scissors and let your imagination run wild. I can promise you that once you begin, the sheer delight of quietly snipping away will take over your life.

Deborah Barker

HAT TRICK

The zebra motif has a clear outline, making it an easy motif for a beginner. Black-and-white always looks stylish and you can keep your hats looking equally hip in this zebra-inspired hatbox. The lid is painted in wavy lines to echo the zebra's unique markings.

YOU WILL NEED
hatbox
latex paint in white and black
large and small paintbrushes
chalk
ruler
small, sharp scissors
white glue
clear water-based acrylic satin varnish

1 Give the hatbox two coats of white latex using a large paintbrush.

2 Paint a band of black latex around the lid using a large paintbrush.

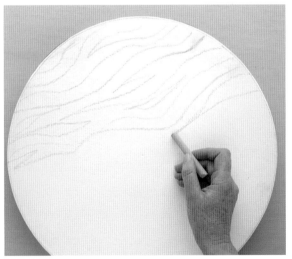

3 When the paint is dry, chalk the zebra stripes on the surface of the hatbox.

4 Paint in the zebra stripes with black paint using a small paintbrush.

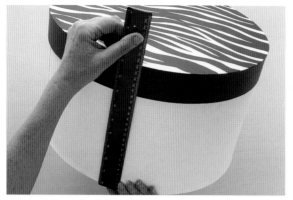

5 Replace the lid and measure from the base of the box to the lip of the lid, and calculate the height of the motif. Allow for a little space above and below each motif.

6 On a photocopier enlarge the zebra motif at the back of the book to your chosen size. Using small, sharp scissors, cut out enough motifs to fit all the way around the box.

7 Position and glue the zebras in place, making sure they are evenly spaced.

8 Cover the lid with two coats of clear satin varnish. Let dry between coats.

9 Varnish the sides of the box and let dry overnight before replacing the lid.

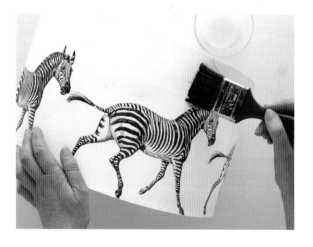

SHELL COLLECTION

Reproductions of old natural history prints are a wonderful source for decoupage images. Simply photocopy as many pictures of shells as desired and use them to decorate a mirror frame. The size of the frame can vary, although it is easier to buy a mirror and make the frame to fit.

YOU WILL NEED

reproductions of shell prints
small, sharp scissors
plain paper
low-tack reusable adhesive
pencil
cardboard
craft knife
cutting mat
ruler
wallpaper paste
newspaper
white latex paint
medium paintbrushes
white glue
hanging fastener
clear water-based acrylic satin varnish

1 Make color photocopies of a selection of reproductions of old shell prints. Carefully cut out the images using small, sharp scissors.

2 Glue the photocopied shells onto a sheet of plain paper using low-tack reusable adhesive and arrange them in a frame shape, slightly overlapping the shells as you work.

3 Draw around the outside and inside edges of the frame with a pencil.

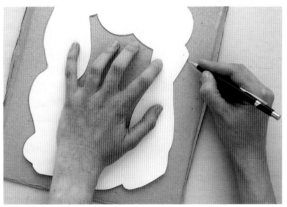

4 Cut out the shape to make a template and place face down on the cardboard. Draw around the edge of the template with a pencil.

11

5 Remove the paper with the shells and cut out the cardboard frame shape using a craft knife and a cutting mat. Also cut out a rectangle and three strips of cardboard for the frame back using a craft knife and ruler.

6 Stick the cardboard strips onto three sides of the cardboard rectangle. Mix up a small amount of the wallpaper paste following the manufacturer's instructions. Dip torn pieces of newspaper into the paste and cover the cardboard with two layers of pasted paper. Let dry.

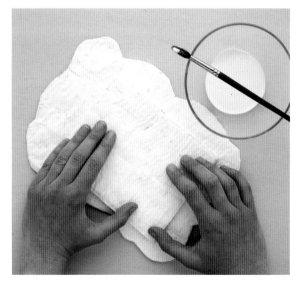

7 Paint the frame front and back with white latex. Glue the frame back to the frame front with white glue. Use heavy books to weight it down.

8 Remove the shells from the paper and glue onto the frame in the same arrangement. Glue a hanging fastener to the back. Apply two coats of varnish.

SCREEN TEST

This screen is decorated with color photocopies of flowers and leaves, and the scope for different colors and shapes is enormous. The combination of delicate gold tissue paper with pretty dried and photocopied flowers is very arresting.

YOU WILL NEED
unpainted screen
parchment-colored matte latex paint
medium paintbrushes
pencil
tape measure
ruler
tissue paper
gold spray paint
wallpaper paste or white glue
scissors
fresh leaves and flowers
craft knife
cutting mat
dried flowers and leaves
stencil cardboard
handmade paper
clear oil- or water-based satin varnish

1 Paint the screen with one coat of parchment-colored matte latex paint, using a medium paintbrush. Let dry completely, then apply a second coat of paint.

2 The screen is decorated with squares of tissue paper, so mark vertical and horizontal guidelines over the screen using a pencil, tape measure and ruler.

3 Spray the sheets of tissue paper with gold paint. Stick down squares of tissue onto the screen using a paintbrush and wallpaper paste or white glue.

4 Cut pieces of tissue paper to fit the curved top edge of the screen and glue in place. Make color photocopies of real leaves and flowers. Carefully cut out the shapes using a craft knife and cutting mat.

5 Select some dried flowers and leaves to decorate the curved top panels of the screen.

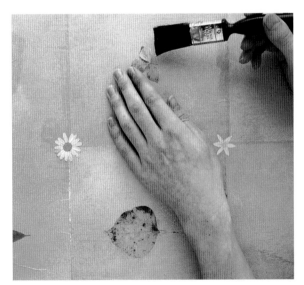

6 Arrange the leaf and flower photocopies on the screen and glue in position.

7 Arrange the dried flowers and leaves on the curved top sections and glue in place.

8 Make a tooth-edged pattern template out of stencil cardboard. Use this to cut out strips of edging from handmade paper.

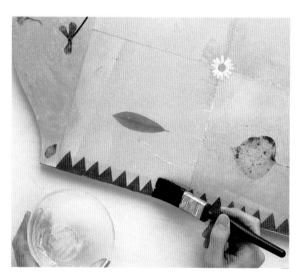

9 Glue the strips to the edges of the screen. When the glue is dry, cover the screen with two coats of satin varnish, letting dry between coats.

VEGE-TABLE

A small table fits in anywhere—in the living room, the kitchen or a study. These chili peppers make a colorful decoration for a table with an easily achieved distressed paint finish. Experiment with different paint colors and decorate with your favorite vegetables.

YOU WILL NEED
wood table
latex paint in white, green and yellow
large and medium paintbrushes
soft cloth
wax
fine-grade sandpaper
tape measure
color pictures of vegetables
craft knife
cutting mat
small, sharp scissors
piece of plastic
white glue
clear water-based acrylic satin varnish

1 Paint the table with white latex paint using a large paintbrush. Let dry. Then paint with green latex and let dry.

2 Using a soft cloth, rub wax unevenly over the surface of the table. Let dry.

3 Paint the table with yellow latex and let dry completely.

4 Using fine-grade sandpaper, gently rub the surface of the table until the green paint is showing through. Sand the surface until the desired distressed look is achieved.

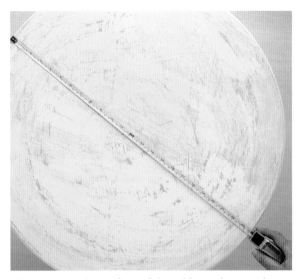

5 Measure the surface of the table so that you know how much to enlarge the vegetables. You may find it helpful to make a newspaper pattern so that you can estimate how many photocopies you need.

6 Photocopy the vegetable pictures. Start by cutting out the small inner areas of the vegetable design using a craft knife and cutting mat. Take care not to tear any of the delicate stems.

7 Cut out larger pieces with a small pair of scissors, taking care not to break the delicate stems.

8 Arrange the vegetables and leaves on the table until you are happy with the design.

9 Pick up the cutouts one at a time and turn upside down onto a piece of plastic to apply the glue. Gently pick up each piece and lay it down on the table, taking care to smooth the surface gently and making sure there are no creases.

10 To finish, varnish with about four coats of clear satin varnish, letting each coat dry before applying the next.

TAKE A LETTER

Many of the images used in decoupage can be found in black-and-white source books. These are photocopied and can then be hand-tinted with paints; the leaves on this letter rack have been given a golden, autumnal hue that is enhanced by the gold leaf.

YOU WILL NEED

unpainted letter rack

green latex paint

medium and small paintbrushes

small, sharp scissors

craft knife

cutting mat

acrylic paint in red, yellow ocher and umber

Japanese gold size

Dutch gold leaf transfer book

soft cloths

white glue

clear water-based acrylic satin varnish

stained wax

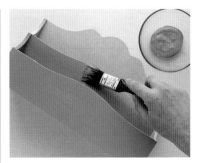

1 Paint the letter rack with green latex paint using a medium paintbrush. Let dry, then apply a second coat of green latex paint.

2 Photocopy the leaves at the back of the book and carefully cut them out. Use small, sharp scissors for the outside edges and a craft knife and cutting mat for the tricky inside areas.

3 Hand-tint the leaves using diluted acrylic paint in red, yellow ocher and umber and a small paintbrush. Use thin washes of color.

4 Paint Japanese gold size onto the top edge of each section of the letter rack. Work over the edge and paint a line roughly the width of your brush. Let dry until the size is still slightly tacky.

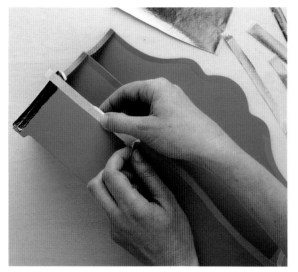

5 Cut the Dutch gold leaf into strips and gently press onto the Japanese gold size. Let dry, then rub off any excess with a dry soft cloth.

6 Arrange the tinted leaves in a pattern on the three sections of the rack and glue in place so that they slightly overlap the gold lines.

7 Varnish with three coats of clear satin varnish, letting the varnish dry thoroughly between each coat.

8 Rub on a thick layer of stained wax, making sure it covers the edges of the paper. Let dry a little, then rub off the wax to leave a nice sheen.

DECOUPAGE DOOR KNOBS

An old chest of drawers can be transformed with a coat of paint and brightly colored knobs. Make the knobs stand out with a different mini-decoupage image for each one. Match the images to the contents of the drawer or just choose pictures that strike your fancy.

YOU WILL NEED
wooden knobs
latex paint in bright colors
small paintbrushes
white glue
imitation gold leaf paper
small, sharp scissors
craft knife
pictures from magazines and wrapping paper
pencil
cutting mat
colored paper
clear water-based acrylic matte varnish
screwdriver and screws

1 Paint each wooden knob in a different color of paint using a small brush. Make a solution of half white glue, half water.

2 For the blue knob, cut a rough square of imitation gold leaf paper with scissors. Pick it up with a craft knife. Brush the surface of the knob with glue and lightly stick the gold paper to the knob. Press down very gently with your finger. Let it dry completely. Cut out a heart and glue it in the center.

3 For the orange knob, draw a set of five rings, one inside the other, on the back of a picture. Using a craft knife and cutting mat, cut out the rings. Apply glue to the knob, then stick the center circle, the middle ring and the outer ring onto the knob with the right side showing.

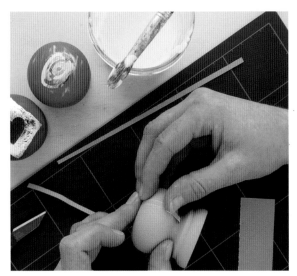

4 For the yellow knob, cut two narrow strips of paper and apply glue to the back. Arrange them at right angles across the knob. Make sure the strips end under the wide part of the knob. Glue a motif to the center to cover the seam.

5 Decorate the remaining knobs with motifs cut from magazines and wrapping paper. Finish with several coats of varnish, letting each coat dry completely before applying the next.

6 Screw the knobs onto your chosen piece of furniture.

Right: The range of options for decorating your door knobs, from swirls and circles to strong graphic images and floral designs, is endless.

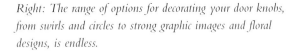

TRAY MAGNIFIQUE

This lovable dog looks very grand surrounded by golden ropes and tassels. This fun project combines decoupage with stenciling techniques. Choose a rich background paint color for the tray to offset the black-and-white photocopy.

YOU WILL NEED
unpainted wood tray
red latex paint
medium and small paintbrushes
scissors
craft knife
cutting mat
white glue
sheet of acetate
permanent black marker
stencil brush
acrylic paint in gold and white
clear water-based acrylic satin varnish
antique pine acrylic varnish

1 Paint the wood tray with red latex paint using a medium paintbrush. Apply a second coat if necessary.

2 Photocopy the dog motif at the back of the book, enlarging it as necessary, and cut out with scissors.

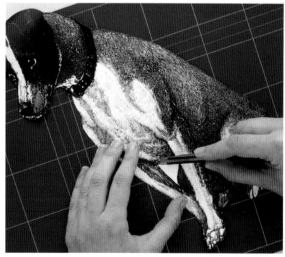

3 Cut out the tricky inner areas using a craft knife and cutting mat.

4 Glue the dog motif in the center of the tray. Let dry.

5 Scale up the cord and tassel templates at the back of the book and draw them onto a sheet of acetate with a permanent black marker.

6 Carefully cut out the stencils with a craft knife and cutting mat.

7 Using a stencil brush and gold acrylic paint, stipple the straight cord stencil all around the edge of the tray to frame the dog, using the corner stencil at each corner.

8 Stencil two tassels in one of the top corners of the tray, and one below the bottom border.

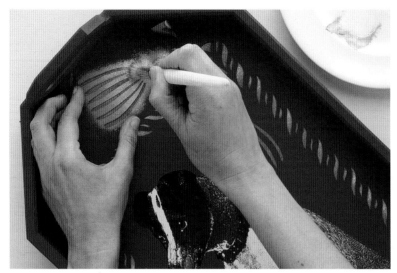

9 Using the same stencils, highlight the cord and tassel with white acrylic paint. Let dry.

10 Finish the tray with three coats of clear acrylic varnish, letting dry completely between coats. Finally, paint on a coat of antique pine acrylic varnish.

DOOR PLAQUE

*It can be difficult to find door plaques, other than plain white ones, to suit contemporary homes.
A clear glass plaque lets you choose any design you like using motifs cut from greeting cards,
wrapping paper or magazines. This quick project is ideal for beginners.*

YOU WILL NEED
clear glass plaque
cardboard
craft knife
cutting mat
ruler
block of wood
masking tape
gold spray paint
pencil
magazine pictures and greeting cards
white glue
clear water-based acrylic satin varnish
screwdriver and screws

1 Cut a rectangle of cardboard slightly bigger than the plaque, using a craft knife, cutting mat and ruler.

2 Tape the rectangle of cardboard onto the wood.

3 Spray with several thin coats of gold paint. Check the manufacturer's instructions — using with a primer gives a much bolder color.

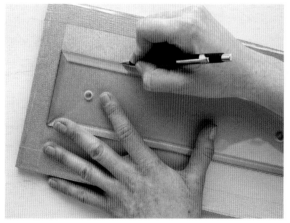

4 Draw a pencil line around the shape of the plaque in the center of the cardboard.

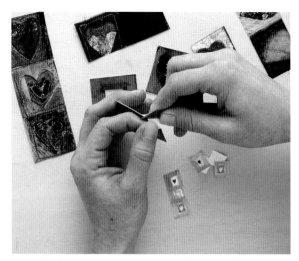

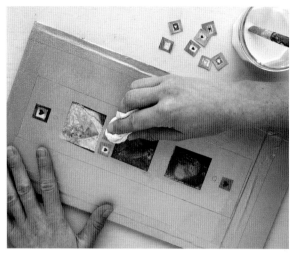

5 If using greeting cards, peel off the thick backing paper with a craft knife to make the paper thinner and easier to work with.

6 Make a solution of half white glue, half water. Arrange the pictures into a pattern on the cardboard panel and glue in place.

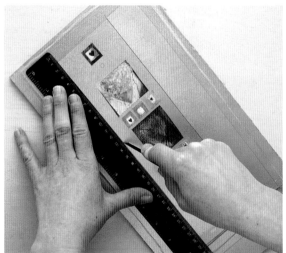

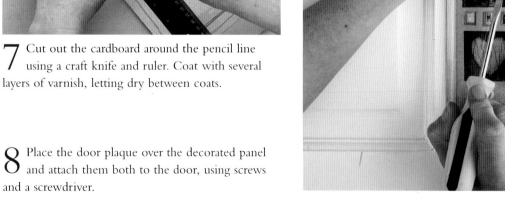

7 Cut out the cardboard around the pencil line using a craft knife and ruler. Coat with several layers of varnish, letting dry between coats.

8 Place the door plaque over the decorated panel and attach them both to the door, using screws and a screwdriver.

FRIEZE FRAME

If you cannot find a wallpaper border that you like, then why not make your own? Just measure the walls of the room and copy as many motifs as you need to fit. Paint the border to match the color of your room for a truly individual look.

YOU WILL NEED
lining paper
ruler
craft knife
yellow latex paint
medium paintbrushes
white glue
small, sharp scissors
green paper
yellow ocher acrylic paint

1 Measure the lining paper to the required length and depth of your frieze. Cut along the edge using a ruler and craft knife.

2 Mix three parts yellow latex paint with one part white glue. Add a little water to let the mixture flow more easily. Use this to paint the lining paper.

3 Photocopy the frieze motifs at the back of the book enough times to cover the length of the border. Cut them out with scissors.

4 Cut the green paper into equal short lengths. Tear along the top edge to represent greenery.

5 Arrange and glue down the buildings and torn paper along the length of the frieze.

6 Glue down the swag motifs along the top edge of the frieze.

7 Mix a little yellow ocher acrylic paint into some white glue. Then dilute four parts tinted glue with one part water.

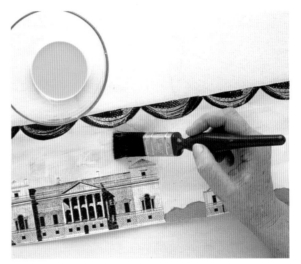

8 Brush the tinted, diluted glue over the frieze to seal and protect it.

STYLE FILE

Turn a plain folder into a work of art using paper scraps and angelic cutouts. The angels are stuck onto layers of colored paper to provide a bold frame. The colored acrylic varnish gives the finished piece a wonderful aged look like that of old leather.

YOU WILL NEED
black folder
ruler
pencil
papers in orange, rust and black
large and small, sharp scissors
white glue
medium paintbrushes
soft cloth
pictures of angels
tinted water-based acrylic satin varnish
craft knife
ribbon

1 Measure the front of the folder and draw a slightly smaller rectangle on orange paper. Tear the paper to size with a ruler to give it a rough edge, and cut off the corners.

2 Measure a rectangle of rust paper, smaller than the orange paper, to make an even margin all around. Use a ruler to tear the paper to size.

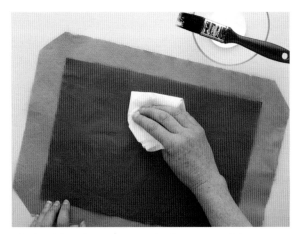

3 Position the rust paper in the center of the orange and glue in place, rubbing it with a soft cloth to smooth out any wrinkles.

4 Spread white glue onto the back of the orange paper. Position and arrange the paper on the folder so that the cut corners allow the corners of the folder to be seen.

5 Cut four strips of black paper to fit inside the orange border and fold into accordions. Draw a diamond shape onto the front panel of each strip. Cut out, leaving a short seam at each folded edge so the diamonds are joined when you open them up.

6 Position and glue the black diamonds along each edge of the folder.

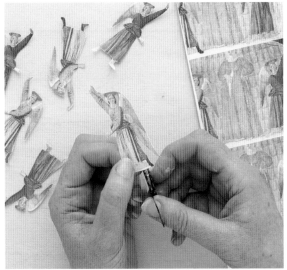

7 Make color photocopies of the angel pictures. Cut out two large angels to go in the center of the folder using small, sharp scissors.

8 Cut out small angels using the small scissors. These will frame the two large angels.

9 Position the angels in the center and around the edge of the folder, and glue in place.

10 Varnish with three or four coats of tinted satin varnish to achieve a leathery look. Finally, make a slit in each side of the folder, close to the edge with a craft knife. Thread a piece of ribbon through each slit from the outside to the inside. Secure with a dab of glue.

ALL SQUARE

An arrangement of simple squares echoing the straight lines of the stool makes this an easy project to attempt. Make sure the pieces of paper are carefully stuck down and varnished to ensure that the stool lives up to the wear and tear of everyday use.

YOU WILL NEED
wood stool with square top
fine- and medium-grade sandpaper
tape measure
pencil
selection of handmade papers
ruler
gold and patterned papers
craft knife
cutting mat
wallpaper paste
medium paintbrushes
clear oil-based satin varnish

1 Sand down the stool using medium-grade then fine-grade sandpaper.

2 Measure the top of the stool and mark the center point with a pencil.

3 Measure four squares of handmade paper to cover the top of the stool. Tear out the paper using a ruler to make the edges slightly uneven.

4 Measure and cut out small squares from gold and patterned papers, using a craft knife, ruler and cutting mat.

5 Mix up a little wallpaper paste according to the manufacturer's instructions. Glue the four large squares of paper onto the stool.

6 When the paper is dry, position the smaller squares on top and glue in place.

7 Measure the edges and sides of the stool and cut pieces of handmade and gold paper to fit. Glue them in place.

8 Position small paper squares around the sides of the stool and glue in place.

9 Work around the stool, making sure all the squares are carefully glued down.

10 When the paste is completely dry, cover with several coats of clear satin varnish.

WASTEBASKET

This wastebasket is appropriately decorated with scraps of paper. Paint the bin in a strong background color, then cut out and arrange a selection of paper shapes to form a pleasing pattern. You will need to use a drill with a metal bit for this project.

YOU WILL NEED
metal wastebasket
mauve eggshell latex paint
medium and small paintbrushes
three wooden knobs (for feet)
drill with metal drill bits
metal file
screwdriver and three screws
natural-colored paper
ruler
craft knife
cutting mat
masking tape
marker
white glue
paper towels
clear oil-based satin varnish

1 Paint the wastebasket with two coats of mauve eggshell latex paint. Let dry.

2 Paint the knobs to match the wastebasket.

3 Drill three holes in the base of the wastebasket and remove any sharp edges with a metal file. Screw the knobs to the base of the wastebasket.

4 Cut narrow strips of paper, using a ruler, craft knife and cutting mat, and arrange them temporarily with pieces of masking tape. ▷

47

5 Using a marker, draw tall triangles on the paper, then cut them out.

6 Glue the diagonal strips of paper onto the wastebasket. Pat in place with paper towels. Trim the ends with a craft knife.

7 Add the paper triangles to the top edge of the wastebasket. Glue a wide strip of paper around the base.

8 Finish with three coats of clear varnish, inside and out, for protection, letting each coat dry before applying the next.

TAKE A SEAT

Create a technicolor dream of a chair using an array of colorful papers. Tear the paper into even pieces, wrap around the chair and glue in place. This rather time-consuming project will certainly attract a lot of attention when it is finished.

YOU WILL NEED

chair
medium-grade sandpaper
wrapping paper
ruler
white glue
small and medium paintbrushes
paper towels
small, sharp scissors
clear oil-based satin varnish
fabric to cover seat
staple gun

1 Sand down the chair with medium-grade sandpaper to provide a surface for the glue.

2 Tear strips of wrapping paper using a ruler, to give soft edges to the strips.

3 Apply plenty of glue to the back of the paper pieces and start to cover the chair.

4 Continue to glue the paper pieces onto the chair, overlapping them very slightly to avoid gaps and bulky seams. Smooth down firmly with some paper towels to remove any air bubbles.

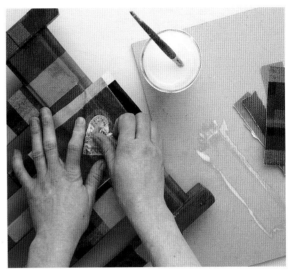

5 Tear strips of paper to fit neatly over any awkward areas. Apply glue to the back of the paper, then, when lightly stuck on, apply more glue over the top of the paper to make it slippery. Slide the paper into position, being careful not to tear it.

6 Choose a strong motif for the focal point of the chair and press down, unglued, with your fingers. Get an imprint of the shape on the chair, then remove and cut out in detail with scissors. Glue in place. Let dry.

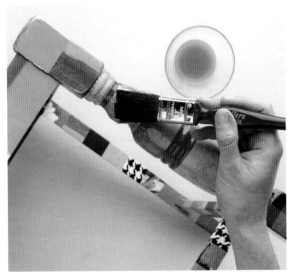

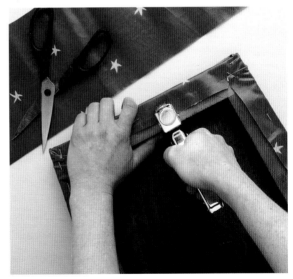

7 Varnish liberally, paying particular attention to the parts that will get the most wear and tear.

8 Cover the chair seat with fabric, securing the edges with a staple gun.

MIRROR MIRROR

A fiberboard mirror frame becomes a work of art when decorated with simple strips of wrapping paper. Apply crackle varnish and gold powder to make it extra special. The variety of techniques necessary for this project makes it suitable for a more experienced craftworker.

YOU WILL NEED
mirror tile and sticky fixer pads
pencil, ruler and felt-tip pen
medium-density fiberboard
jigsaw and protective mask
wood glue
wrapping paper
craft knife
cutting mat
white glue
small and medium paintbrushes
spray adhesive
crackle varnish
gold powder
soft cloth
spray fixative
clear oil-based satin varnish
drill with wood drill bits
string
picture rings and chain
screwdriver

1 Draw around the mirror tile onto the fiberboard and add a 3½-inch border all around. Cut a back and a front panel to this size using a jigsaw. Cut out the center of the front panel. Cut a 3¼ x 7-inch plaque. (Always wear a mask when cutting fiberboard because of the fine dust it creates.) Glue the panels together using wood glue.

2 Cut strips of wrapping paper in varying widths using a craft knife, ruler and cutting mat and arrange them on the frame front. Glue in place with white glue.

3 To make each corner piece, hold a piece of paper onto the frame and press around the edges. Remove and cut out the corner section. Glue the back of the paper and fold over the edges of the frame.

4 Draw two decorative swirls on the back of the paper with a felt-tip pen. Cut out using a craft knife and cutting mat.

5 Place the swirls on a piece of scrap paper and spray with adhesive. Glue onto two corners of the frame.

6 Apply two coats of crackle varnish, following the manufacturer's instructions, to give a crackle finish to the frame.

7 Rub gold powder into the cracks with a cloth, using small amounts at a time. Rub off any excess. Seal the frame with fixative. Decorate the hanging plaque in the same way as the frame. Coat both the frame and the hanging plaque with varnish. ▶

8 Drill two holes in the bottom of the frame and in the top of the hanging plaque. Attach the two together with string, knotting the ends at the front.

9 Stick the mirror in place using sticky pads.

10 Attach the picture rings and chain to the back.

WOOD BOX

This beautiful box can be used for storing special photographs, letters and mementos. Choose faces and lettering from wrapping paper or prints and combine with a collage of handmade paper scraps in varying colors. The finished box is color washed to give it an aged look.

YOU WILL NEED
wood box
fine-grade sandpaper
reproductions of "old master" drawings of
faces, animals and lettering
tracing paper
pencil
handmade uncolored Japanese paper
carbon paper
wallpaper paste or white glue
small, medium and large paintbrushes
watercolor paints
magazine pictures
scissors
stencil cardboard
ruler
craft knife
cutting mat
decorator's sponge
burnt umber acrylic paint
clear oil-based matte varnish

1 Sand the box with fine-grade sandpaper to get a smooth surface, and clean the metal hinges and catches of the box.

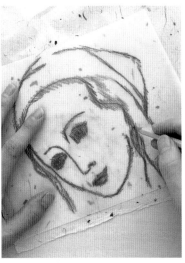

2 Make photocopies of reproductions of "old master" drawings. Trace over the images and transfer them onto pieces of handmade paper.

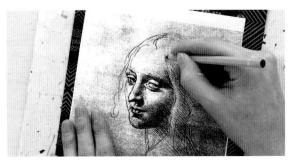

3 Alternatively, you can photocopy the image and place carbon paper face down on the handmade paper. Draw over the image so that the tracing comes through onto the handmade paper.

4 When you have traced a selection of images, tear them out roughly. Also tear up some plain handmade paper into irregular pieces. Arrange the images on the box.

5 Glue down the pieces, completely covering the surface of the box. Make colored photocopies of different types of lettering. Glue photocopies of old parchment onto the box, too.

6 Handpaint some motifs of your own, to add touches of color and interest. Let dry, then cut roughly or tear around these images and glue onto the box.

7 Glue on any other details cut or photocopied from color magazines.

8 Design and cut out a stencil pattern for the edges from stencil cardboard, using a craft knife and cutting mat.

9 Use a sponge to stencil the border pattern onto handmade paper with water-color paint.

10 Enhance the images on the box with touches of watercolor paints and wash over the entire surface with an antiquing color such as diluted burnt umber acrylic paint.

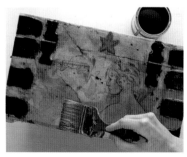

11 Finish with a coat of clear matte varnish.

STILL LIFE

Classic Dutch tulips captured in a still life have a timeless appeal. Create your own decoupage flower arrangement and preserve it forever on a small box, a table top or a tray. The design is simple but some care is needed to apply the pieces accurately.

YOU WILL NEED
small cardboard box with lid
latex paint in white and yellow
medium and small paintbrushes
reproduction of an old flower print
small, sharp scissors
white glue
green paper
ruler
craft knife
cutting mat
clear water-based acrylic satin varnish

1 Paint the box and lid with white latex and let dry. Next, paint it with two coats of yellow latex.

2 Make color photocopies of the print and carefully cut out the flowers using a pair of small, sharp scissors.

3 Arrange the flowers on the lid. Keep the stems close together to form a bunch. Glue them down using a small brush to apply the glue.

4 Cut out a rectangle of green paper. Fold it in half lengthwise and then in half again. Using a small pair of scissors, cut three small triangles from the folded edge. Open out the paper and glue in place on the lid to form a vase.

5 To match up the flowers on the edge of the lid and the sides of the box, hold each flower against the lid and press to make a crease.

6 Cut along the crease with a craft knife and cutting mat, using a ruler as a guide.

7 Glue the flower onto the edge of the lid, then line up the flower on the box side and glue in place. Add more flowers around the box.

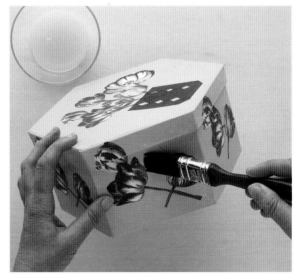

8 Varnish the finished box with three or four coats of clear satin varnish, letting dry completely between coats.

COAT RACK

This contemporary design, using images taken from books, magazines and posters, is perfect for children's rooms. Woodworking skills are needed to make the rack, although you could simply decorate a ready-made rack. Let each child create their own montage.

YOU WILL NEED

3/8-inch thick medium-density fiberboard
ruler
pencil
jigsaw and a protective mask
duck-egg blue latex paint
medium and small paintbrushes
magazine pictures
craft knife
cutting mat
plain colored paper
white glue
three wooden knobs
silver acrylic paint
drill and wood drill bits
screwdriver and three countersunk screws
clear water-based acrylic matte varnish
two mirror plates and screws

1 Following the diagram at the back of the book, draw out the shape of the coat rack on fiberboard with a ruler and pencil. Cut out using a jigsaw.

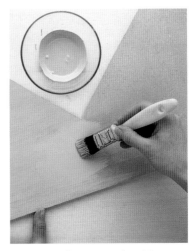

2 Paint the coat rack with two coats of duck-egg blue latex, letting the paint dry completely between coats.

3 Cut out pictures from magazines using a craft knife and cutting mat.

4 Cut three 4-inches in diameter circles of plain paper. Glue the backs and position them along the base of the rack below each point.

5 Arrange the motifs on the rack and, when you are happy with the arrangement, stick them down. Start with your favorite images and arrange the rest to complement them.

6 Paint the knobs with silver acrylic paint and let dry.

7 Drill three holes in the rack, one through the center of each paper circle. Countersink the holes on the back of the rack. Use countersunk screws to attach the knobs to the rack. Varnish the complete rack and let dry.

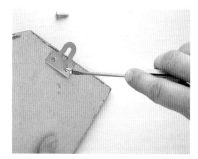

8 Attach a mirror plate to each end of the back of the rack.

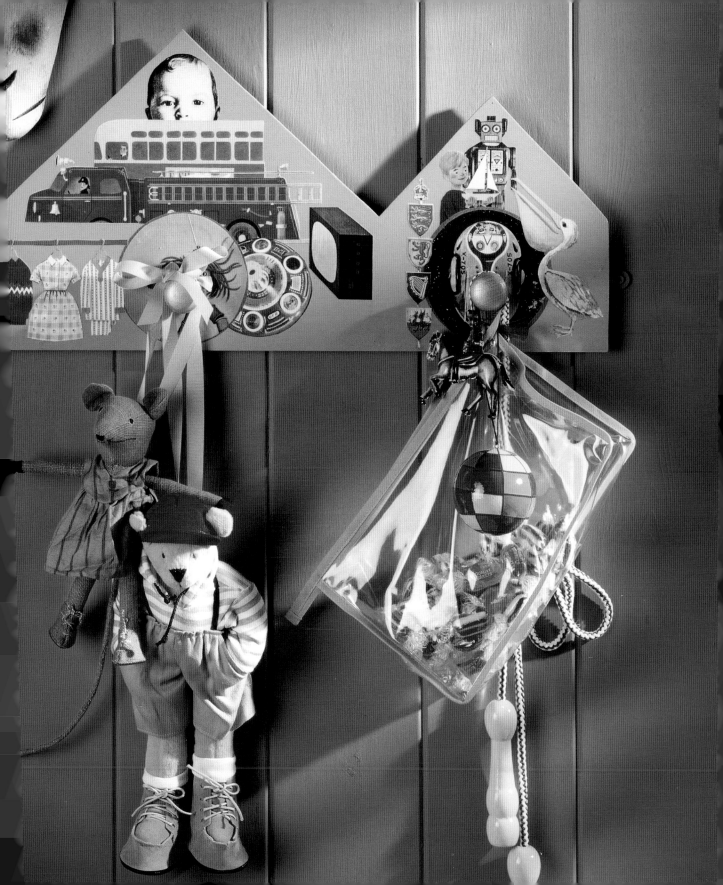

PLACE SETTINGS

Decorate new unpainted mats or renovate worn ones with a paint effect and decoupage decoration. The background creates the impression of raw silk to complement the Chinese print. The rather time-consuming techniques will provide beautiful results for the more advanced decoupage artist.

YOU WILL NEED
set of place mats
water-based traditional paint in bright blue and pale green
medium and small paintbrushes
clear water-based acrylic dead-flat varnish
glaze medium
paper towels
photocopy of a Chinese print
white French polish
craft knife
cutting mat
small, sharp scissors
pencil
paper glue
permanent ink gold pen
shellac
clear satin varnish
gold wax
clear polyurethane matte varnish

1 Paint the surface of each mat with quick-drying water-based traditional paint in bright blue using sideways strokes. Let dry, then seal with dead-flat water-based varnish.

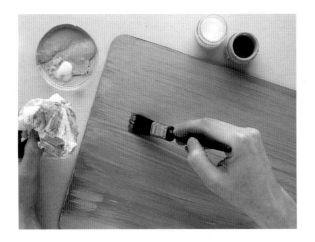

2 Using pale green traditional paint mixed with a little glaze medium, paint over the whole surface of the mat using sideways strokes again. With a paper towel wipe away some areas in the direction of the brushstrokes. The aim is to give the impression of raw silk. The glaze will slow down the drying and give you time to experiment. When you are satisfied with the results, let dry. Seal with dead-flat acrylic varnish.

3 Seal the colored Chinese print with white French polish using paper towels. Carefully cut out the motifs with a craft knife, and then cut around the outside of the shape with small scissors. In order to avoid tearing, small details, such as the righthand basket, can be cut off and reattached at the gluing stage.

4 Decide where the print is to go, lightly mark with a pencil and then apply paper glue to this area of the mat. Work the glue over the surface with your finger so that it forms an even film. Position the print and gently rub it with your finger to make sure it is well in place. Check that there are no air bubbles or wrinkles. Let dry overnight and then remove all extra glue from the surface.

5 Photocopy the border motifs from the back of the book. Color in the border motifs with gold pen and seal with shellac. Let dry and carefully cut out with a craft knife, cutting the center areas first. Glue the corner pieces to the mat, 1 inch from the edge. (If you are planning to decorate a whole set of mats, it is a good idea to make a border template from 1-inch-wide strips of paper to prevent constant measuring.)

6 Draw a gold line around the edge of the mat using the curved corner of another mat as a template. Cover with up to 12 coats of clear satin varnish, letting it dry between coats.

7 Rub gold wax around the edge of the mat and then apply two coats of clear matte varnish over the whole mat to make it heatproof.

Above: Use the same techniques to create a set of differently decorated mats using your own choice of motifs and borders.

CANDLE SHADES

These delicate-looking shades, made from Japanese handmade paper and photocopies of real leaves and flowers, match the soft glow of candlelight. They are treated with fire-proofing spray, but for extra safety, do not leave them unattended when lit.

YOU WILL NEED
Japanese handmade paper
clear oil-based dead-flat varnish
medium and small paintbrushes
compass
ruler
pencil
cardboard
scissors
selection of fresh and dried flowers
and leaves
craft knife
cutting mat
masking tape
wallpaper paste or white glue
decorative paper
fire-proofing spray
candle
candlestick

1 Varnish the handmade paper with clear dead–flat varnish and let dry.

2 Using a compass, a ruler and a pencil, draw the shape of the shade onto cardboard, following the design shown in the photograph. Cut out to use as a template. It is a good idea to make a trial shade out of newspaper.

3 Draw around the cardboard template onto the handmade paper and cut out.

4 Make color photocopies of the flowers and leaves. Carefully cut them out using a craft knife and cutting mat.

5 To plan your design, arrange the cutouts on the handmade paper, securing them temporarily with masking tape. Glue them in place.

6 Cut out edging details from strips of decorative paper and glue them in place. Leave space at the seam edge. Once the shade is made up, you can add extra pieces to cover the seam.

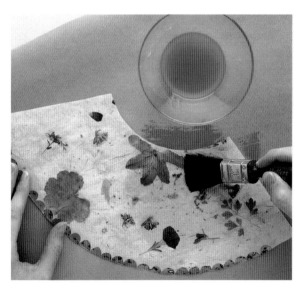

7 Cover the shade with a coat of clear varnish. Let dry, then glue the shade together.

8 Draw around the circumference on a piece of cardboard to make the shade support.

9 In the center of the support, draw a smaller circle for the candle to fit through. Draw intersecting lines through this circle. Then mark four more holes to let air circulate. Cut out the support and the small circles.

10 Spray the shade with fireproofing spray.

11 Push the candle through the cardboard support onto the candlestick. Place the shade over the candle to rest on the support.

WALL OF COLOR

This colorful checkerboard wall is simply painted with steel wool pads before being embellished with cut-out plates and vases. Cheaper than buying all that china — and totally unbreakable, too. This is not a difficult design and can be attempted by a beginner.

YOU WILL NEED
white glue
lining paper (or work directly on the wall)
medium and small paintbrushes
white latex paint
blue acrylic paint
two steel wool pads
pictures of plates and vases
small, sharp scissors

1 Dilute four parts white glue with one part water. Brush onto the lining paper or wall to seal the surface.

2 Paint with white latex and let dry.

3 On a plate, mix a little blue acrylic paint into the white latex to make a pale blue.

4 Using two wool pads, one as a spacer and the other for applying the paint, print a checkerboard pattern over the wall or paper. Practice the technique on a piece of scrap paper first.

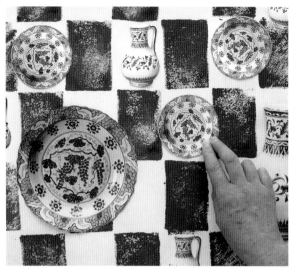

5 Make color photocopies of pictures of plates and vases in different sizes and carefully cut them out with small, sharp scissors.

6 Arrange the photocopies on the checkered background.

7 Glue them in position with the diluted white glue. Carefully smooth down the motifs, working from the center to the edges.

8 Seal the finished design with the diluted white glue to protect the wall.

SHELF LIFE

Bring interest to a forgotten corner with a boldly colored shelf unit that is easy to decorate. The painted cream- and brown-striped shelves go beautifully with the vase and urn motifs, which are reproductions from a painting by Goya, and are perfect for displaying your own artifacts.

YOU WILL NEED
wooden shelf unit
latex paint in white, cream and chocolate
medium and small paintbrushes
fine-grade sandpaper
pencil
ruler
pictures of pitchers and vases
large and small, sharp scissors
white glue
clear water-based acrylic satin varnish

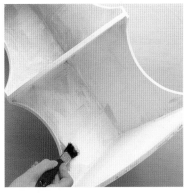

1 Paint the shelf unit with two coats of white latex, sanding it between the coats.

2 When dry, paint with two coats of cream latex.

3 Make faint pencil lines before painting in the chocolate stripes using an artist's brush. Steady your hand by resting it on the edge of the shelf.

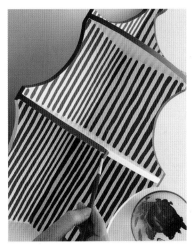

4 Paint the edges of the shelf unit with the same chocolate-brown paint.

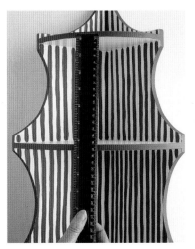

5 Measure the shelves to gauge the correct height of the photocopies. Make color photocopies of pitchers and vases. ▶

6 Cut out the pitchers and vases using large scissors for the outer edges and small scissors for the inside details.

7 Arrange the pitchers and vases on the shelf unit, overlapping them a little but without overcrowding the images.

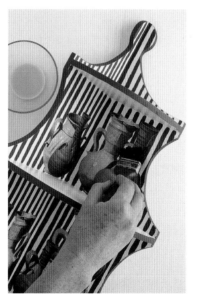

8 Glue down the first layer of pitchers and vases, then glue down the second layer.

9 Finish the shelf with three or four coats of clear acrylic satin varnish.

KEY MATTERS

You will never lose another key with this sophisticated cupboard to store them in. The cupboard is given a subtle distressed look before finishing with a decorative print. The monkey holding the key is achieved by cutting and cleverly repositioning the image.

YOU WILL NEED

unpainted wood key cupboard
medium-grade sandpaper
shellac knotting
medium and small paintbrushes
shellac or sanding sealer
water-based traditional paint in deep red and deep blue
clear water-based acrylic dead-flat varnish
candle
fine steel wool
ruler
photocopies of script
craft knife
cutting mat
paper glue
watercolor paints
small, sharp scissors
clear water-based acrylic satin varnish
wax polish and paper towels

1 Sand down any rough wood on the cupboard and apply shellac knotting over any knots. Seal the surface with shellac or sanding sealer. Paint the cupboard inside and out with deep red traditional paint and let dry. Then seal the surface with a coat of dead-flat varnish.

2 Rub candle wax over the areas where there would be natural wear and tear, such as under the key hole and around the edges of the door, to create a resist.

3 Brush over the outside of the box only in deep blue paint using loose brushstrokes. When the paint is completely dry, rub over with fine steel wool. The blue paint will come off over the waxed areas, revealing the red paint underneath.

4 Measure the center panel on the door and cut a piece of script to this size. Glue in place, checking that there are no air bubbles and that the edges are firmly glued down. Let dry overnight. Seal the panel with a coat of dead–flat varnish.

5 Photocopy the key and monkey motifs at the back of the book. Using watercolor paints, tint the monkey with raw umber, deepening some areas to create shadowing. Tint the keys with yellow ocher. Seal all the prints on both sides with white shellac.

6 Choose which key prints you are going to to use inside the box. Cut out, starting with the delicate areas using a craft knife, then use scissors for the outer edges. Arrange the keys inside the box, positioning them about ¼ inch below where the hooks for the real keys will go. Glue in place by applying the glue to the surface of the box and gently spreading the glue with your finger. Place each key on top and smooth it down, checking that all parts are well in place.

7 Cut out the monkey print. If he is to appear to hold the key, cut off the left hand and set it aside. Choose a suitable key and cut it in half. Glue the monkey to the panel and smooth out with your finger. Glue the key to the panel, positioning it on either side of the hand to make it look realistic. Let dry.

hundred and thirty seven
and on the South by
Street called
to all the rights of the Lord of the
part of the said William

8 Clean off any extra glue. Paint over the prints with up to twelve coats of clear satin varnish, allowing two hours drying time between coats. Wax with a good-quality wax polish.

Above: Decoupage is a delightful way of assembling images. Here, the bird and butterfly are made to sit on the branch.

MATERIALS

The materials needed for decoupage are inexpensive and readily available at arts and crafts stores. The basic items are listed here; more specialized requirements are given in the lists of materials for individual projects.

CUTTINGS

Images for decoupage can be gleaned from many sources, such as wrapping paper, prints, newspapers, greeting cards and catalogs. They can be photo-copied in black-and-white and color washed in your own choice of colors, or color copied to make endless duplicates for a frieze or set of mats. Start a collection of decoupage images, motifs and pictures that catch your eye so you will always have a store of cuttings from which to choose.

GLUES

Paper glue is a golden-colored liquid glue that comes in a bottle. It is ideal for paper projects, although it may be slower to dry than other glues.

White glue is a glue that dries quickly to a clear finish. It can be used full strength or diluted as required (see individual project instructions). It can also be diluted to use as a sealer on finished decoupage projects.

Wood glue may be required for some of the projects involving woodwork. It is a stronger form of white glue.

Spray adhesive gives a light, even application of glue. Always work in a well-ventilated area when using this type of glue.

Wallpaper paste is easy to mix up and use for larger projects, but it is not as strong as white glue. It contains fungicide, which prevents mold. It has a slippery feel, ideal for moving the decoupage motifs into an accurate position.

PAINTS

Acrylic paints come in a range of colors. Ideal for applying color highlights, acrylic paints can be used full strength or diluted with water or an acrylic medium. Mixing with an acrylic medium gives a stronger color.

Latex paints are used for most of the projects in this book. They come in a wide variety of colors and dry quickly.

Traditional paints come in a range of subtle colors and dry to a chalky finish similar to the old-fashioned casein or milk paints. They need sealing with a coat of acrylic varnish before the next coat is applied.

VARNISHES

These are available as oil-based polyurethane varnishes or water-based acrylic varnishes. Both types are available in gloss, satin (mid-sheen) or matte finishes. Acrylic varnish has the advantage of not yellowing with age.

Shellac dries to a transparent finish. It is less hardwearing than varnish and tends to be used between layers rather than as a finishing sealer.

OTHER MATERIALS

Masking tape is used for screening off areas before painting and also for temporarily attaching the motifs while arranging them.

Wood filler is necessary for filling any holes in furniture or other wooden items before applying the decoupage motifs. Sand down the dried filler to ensure a smooth surface.

Turpentine is a clear solvent used for diluting oil-based paints, washing brushes and cleaning objects to be decoupaged.

Spiraling from top left: traditional paints, acrylic paints, acrylic varnish, wallpaper paste, masking tape, shellac, cuttings, paper glue, wood glue, wood filler, turpentine, oil-based varnish, latex paint and white glue.

EQUIPMENT

Apart from a pair of small, sharp scissors and a selection of paintbrushes in different sizes, there are very few pieces of equipment that are needed for decoupage projects. Where woodworking techniques are needed to make the base of a project, the extra equipment is listed.

PAINTBRUSHES

The key to good paintwork is choosing the correct paintbrush. The three main types of brushes are household or decorator's, artist's and stencil brushes, and each type comes in a wide variety of shapes and sizes.

Household brushes should be used for painting basecoats and applying varnishes, and artist's brushes for fine paintwork. You can buy specialty varnishing brushes, although household ones are perfectly adequate.

Artist's brushes are used for hand-tinting prints and adding intricate decoration.

Stencil brushes are used when a decoupage project also uses stenciled images.

Always ensure that a different brush is used for the varnish and the paintwork, otherwise the varnish will have flecks of paint in it.

Buy the best-quality paintbrush you can or the work may be spoiled by loose hairs caught in the varnish.

Clean brushes immediately after use; clean them in water if the paint or varnish is water-based or in turpentine if the paint or varnish is oil-based.

CUTTING EQUIPMENT

For decoupage, you will need a pair of small, sharp scissors to cut around intricate motifs and a pair of larger scissors for cutting out templates and larger pieces of paper and cardboard.

Some people prefer to use a scalpel or craft knife as these are particularly good for cutting out intricate patterns. The blades are extremely sharp; they should always be used with a cutting mat so that the knife does not slip or damage your work surface. Replace the blade regularly so that it remains sharp and gives you a good, clean outline.

OTHER EQUIPMENT

Sandpaper comes in various grades from fine to coarse. Use a fine-grade paper for rubbing down between coats of paint and use a coarser paper for preparing surfaces before you begin your decoupage.

Tweezers are useful for picking up very delicate cutouts, which may get damaged in your fingers.

Metal rulers are essential if you are cutting along a straight edge with a utility knife because the blade will make nicks in a plastic ruler and then the line will not be straight. Metal rulers are also useful for cutting paper when you want a softer edge than can be made by scissors. A metal or plastic ruler can be used for measuring and designing projects.

A compass is sometimes needed for designing projects.

A pencil or felt-tip pen and paper are needed for planning designs and marking the positions of cutouts.

Soft cloths, paper towels and dish towels are useful for rubbing down images and removing excess glue from the surface.

Access to a black-and-white and a color photocopier is also very useful because you may need to make large numbers of copies.

Clockwise from top left: cutting mat, tweezers, scalpel, utility knife, compass, metal ruler, tape measure, plastic ruler, felt-tip pen, pencil, stencil brush, artist's paintbrushes, household paintbrushes, soft cloth, dish towel, paper towel, medium-grade and fine-grade sandpaper, large scissors and small, sharp scissors.

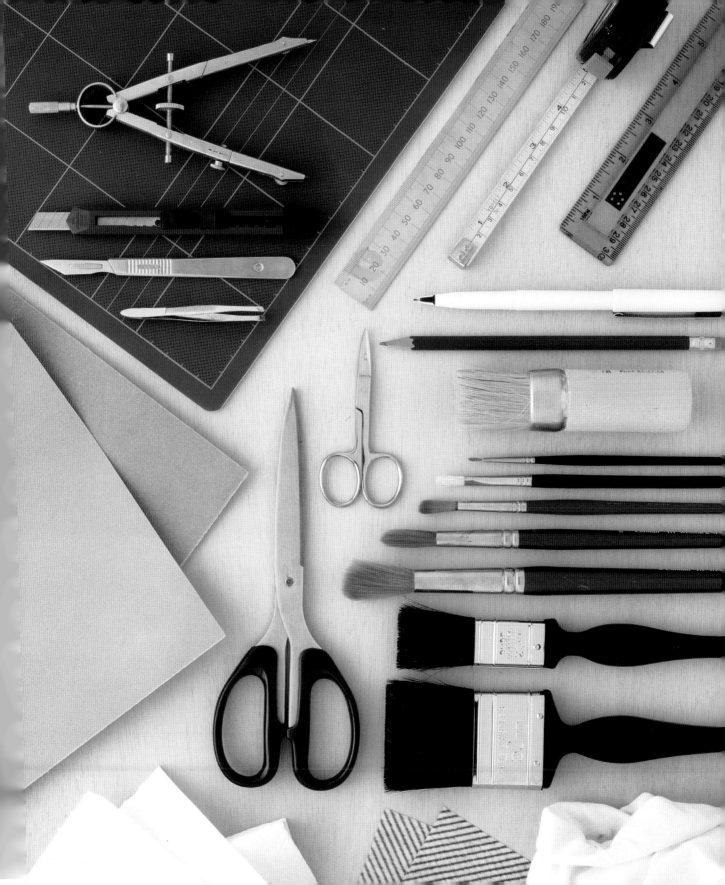

TECHNIQUES

The techniques of decoupage are very simple and are quickly learned. The most important skill is that of carefully cutting out and handling the paper cutting. The project shown here covers all the basic processes involved in decoupage.

PREPARING SURFACES

1 For older and worn wood items, it is essential to wipe the surface with turpentine, then fill any nicks with wood filler, following the manufacturer's instructions.

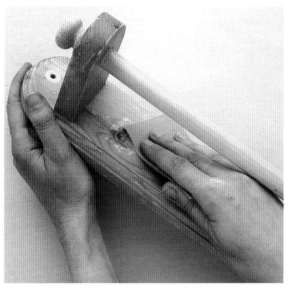

2 Sand down the object with sandpaper until smooth and seal with shellac.

3 Wipe away any dust with turpentine so that you have a clean surface.

4 Prime the object with two coats of white latex paint. An additional color can then be painted on top.

SEALING

CUTTING

5 Seal the image with a coat of shellac painted onto the paper. The images may be wrapping paper, color or black–and–white photocopies or prints. Shellac also stiffens delicate images, making them easier to cut out and preventing discoloration.

6 Cut roughly around the image with a pair of large scissors.

7 Then cut around the edge of the image with a smaller pair of scissors. For delicate images, hold the paper in your hand and rotate it as you cut the curves. Always use a ruler to tear straight edges.

8 To cut out internal unwanted paper, use a craft knife and cutting mat. Always take care when using a craft knife.

STICKING

  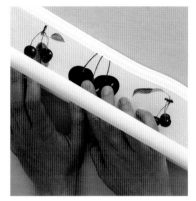

9 Hold and arrange your cut-out images on the painted surface with blobs of low-tack reusable adhesive. This lets you try different arrangements without damaging and wasting your images.

10 When you are happy with the positioning, glue the motifs onto the background using white glue diluted with a little water.

11 Use a pair of tweezers to pick up delicate images. Place in position, press down and rub with your fingers or a soft cloth to get rid of any air bubbles or excess glue. Wipe off any excess glue with a damp cloth. Let dry.

VARNISHING

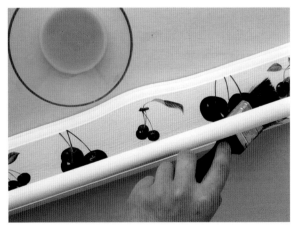 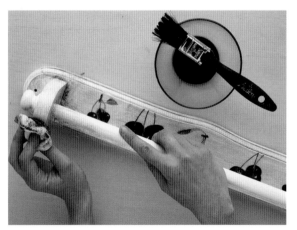

12 Varnishing is the final protection. Acrylic varnish is faster-drying and less toxic than oil-based varnish. Seal your finished design with up to twelve coats of clear varnish, giving it a light sanding between coats. The object must be left to dry in a dust-free atmosphere so that it does not pick up any dust particles.

13 Finally, to age an object and to blend the colors, paint on a stained varnish such as antique pine or oak. To get rid of any brushstrokes, rub off the excess stain with a clean cloth, lightly dabbed all over. You can then use a wax polish to give a deep satin feel to the finished piece.

TEMPLATES

All black-and-white images or images to be color washed that are used in the projects in this book are provided here. You will need to source color images yourself. Always measure the object to be decorated and calculate the enlargement necessary before photocopying.

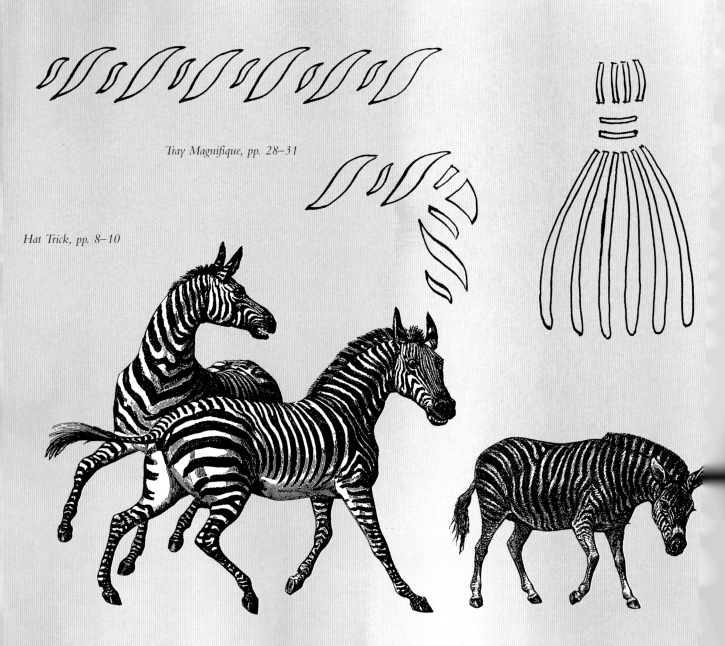

Tray Magnifique, pp. 28–31

Hat Trick, pp. 8–10

Key Matters, pp. 80–83

Take a Letter, pp. 23–24

Tray Magnifique, pp. 28–31

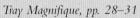

Place Settings,
pp. 66–69

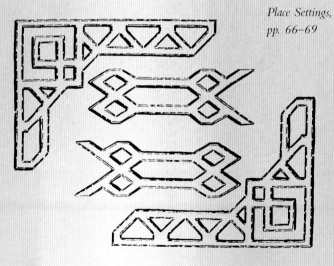

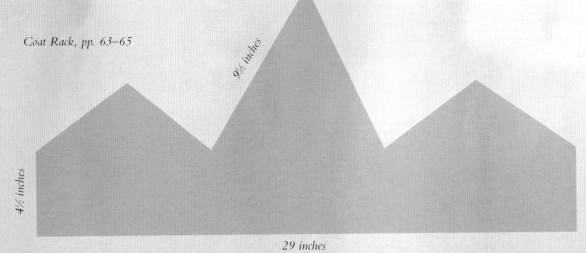

Coat Rack, pp. 63–65

9½ inches

4½ inches

29 inches

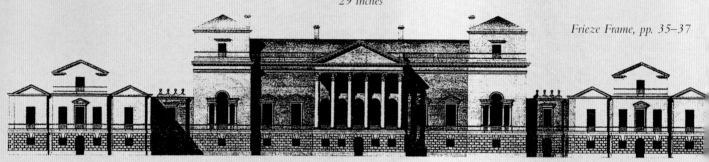

Frieze Frame, pp. 35–37

Key Matters, pp. 80–83

SUPPLIERS

Decoupage requires very few specialty materials. The glues, varnishes and paints are available at any good arts supply store.

The sources of decorative images for decoupage are endless: glossy magazines, postcards, gift cards, books and newspapers. Listed below are a few specialty suppliers. Museums are a wonderful source of books and postcards with reproductions of famous paintings and prints. Interior decorating stores also sell a good range of print material.

The Art Store
935 Erie Blvd. E.
Syracuse, NY 13210
Tel: (315) 474-1000

Dick Blick
P. O. Box 1267
Galesburg, IL 61402
Tel: (309) 343-6181

Dover Publications Inc.
31 East 2nd Street
Mineola, NY 11501
Tel: (516) 294-7000

Joe Kubert Art & Graphic Supply
37A Myrtle Avenue
Dover, NJ 07801
Tel: (201) 328-3266

National Artcraft Co.
23456 Mercantile Road
Beachwood, OH 44122
Tel: (216) 963-6011

S & S Arts & Crafts
P. O. Box 513
Colchester, CT 06415
Tel: (800) 243-9232

Zimmerman's
2884 35th Street N.
St. Petersurg, FL 33713
Tel: (813) 526-4880

ACKNOWLEDGMENTS

The publishers would like to thank the following people for designing the projects in this book: Catherine Macdonald for the Hat Trick, pp. 8–10, Vege-Table, pp. 18–21, Frieze Frame, pp. 35–7, Style File, pp. 38–41, Still Life, pp. 60–2, Wall of Color, pp. 74–6, Shelf Life, pp. 77–9; Josephine Whitfield for the Shell Collection, pp. 11–13, Take a Letter, pp. 22–4, Tray Magnifique, pp. 28–31 and the Techniques; Kerry Skinner of Rare Creation for the Screen Test, pp. 14–17, All Square, pp. 42–5, Wood Box, pp. 56–9 and Candle Shades, pp. 70–3; Sandra Hadfield for the Decoupage Door Knobs, pp. 25–7, Door Plaque, pp. 32–4, Wastebasket, pp. 46–8, Take a Seat, pp. 49–51, Mirror Mirror, pp. 52–5 and Coat Rack, pp. 63–5; Elaine Green for Place Settings, pp. 66–9 and Key Matters, pp. 80–93.

INDEX